D1709501

YOSEMITE
National Park

BY CHRISTINA LEAF

BLASTOFF!
DISCOVERY

BELLWETHER MEDIA • MINNEAPOLIS, MN

Blastoff! Discovery launches a new mission: reading to learn. Filled with facts and features, each book offers you an exciting new world to explore!

BLASTOFF! UNIVERSE

GRADE
K

GRADES
1-3

GRADE
4

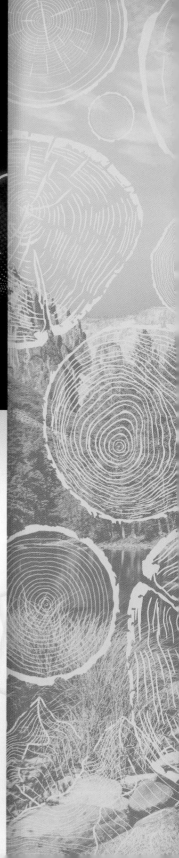

This edition first published in 2023 by Bellwether Media, Inc.

No part of this publication may be reproduced in whole or in part without written permission of the publisher.
For information regarding permission, write to Bellwether Media, Inc.,
Attention: Permissions Department,
6012 Blue Circle Drive, Minnetonka, MN 55343.

Library of Congress Cataloging-in-Publication Data

Names: Leaf, Christina, author.
Title: Yosemite National Park / by Christina Leaf.
Description: Minneapolis : Bellwether Media, 2023. |
    Series: Blastoff! Discovery: U.S. national parks | Includes bibliographical
    references and index. | Audience: Ages 7-13 | Audience: Grades 4-6 |
    Summary: "Engaging images accompany information about Yosemite
    National Park. The combination of high-interest subject matter and narrative
    text is intended for students in grades 3 through 8"– Provided by publisher.
Identifiers: LCCN 2022016483 (print) | LCCN 2022016484 (ebook) |
    ISBN 9781644877579 (library binding) | ISBN 9781648348037 (ebook)
Subjects: LCSH: Yosemite National Park (Calif.)–Juvenile literature.
Classification: LCC F868.Y6 L38 2023 (print) | LCC F868.Y6 (ebook) |
    DDC 979.4/47–dc23/eng/20220414
LC record available at https://lccn.loc.gov/2022016483
LC ebook record available at https://lccn.loc.gov/2022016484

Editor: Betsy Rathburn
Series Design: Jeffrey Kollock   Book Designer: Laura Sowers

Printed in the United States of America, North Mankato, MN.

TABLE OF CONTENTS

VERNAL FALL

It is a sunny summer day as a family begins their hike.
They walk on a wooded trail along the clear Merced River.
They cross the river and catch a glimpse of a rushing waterfall
tumbling over a gray rock wall. It is Vernal Fall!

MERCED RIVER

MOONBOWS

Yosemite is famous for its moonbows! These nighttime rainbows can appear near waterfalls on clear nights when the moon is full.

The family stops to put on raincoats. Then, they follow the trail up a slick stone staircase right next to the waterfall. The spray from the falls soaks the hikers! As they climb to the top, a rainbow appears at the bottom of the falls. This is the beautiful Yosemite National Park!

YOSEMITE NATIONAL PARK

Yosemite National Park is known for towering rock formations and amazing waterfalls. It is one of the country's oldest national parks! The park lies in east-central California in the Sierra Nevada mountain range. It covers 1,190 square miles (3,082 square kilometers).

The Merced River flows through Yosemite Valley, the most famous part of the park. To the south lies a stand of giant sequoia trees in Mariposa Grove. The high **alpine** area of Tuolumne Meadows lies northeast of the Valley. Hetch Hetchy Valley lies in the northwest.

HETCH HETCHY VALLEY

TUOLUMNE MEADOWS

YOSEMITE VALLEY

MERCED RIVER

MARIPOSA GROVE

CALIFORNIA

PACIFIC OCEAN

N
W E
S

⬛ = YOSEMITE NATIONAL PARK

MARIPOSA GROVE

HETCH HETCHY VALLEY

7

THE LAND

HALF DOME

The Yosemite area was originally covered in **sedimentary** rock. Some of this rock became **metamorphic** from heat and pressure. Later, areas of underground melted rock were pushed up into the layers of sedimentary and metamorphic rock. These events are known as **intrusions**. The melted rock cooled slowly underground, forming granite. Millions of years of **erosion** eventually uncovered the granite. The park's most famous granite intrusion is Half Dome.

Around 2 to 3 million years ago, **glaciers** formed in Yosemite's mountains. A glacier moved through the narrow valley cut by the Merced River. This rounded the valley into a U shape. The glacier left behind lakes and rivers.

HOW INTRUSIONS FORM

1. Melted rock pushes rock layers up.

2. Melted rock cools and becomes granite.

melted rock

granite

3. Wind and rain erode softer outer layers.

4. Granite is uncovered.

The mountains of Yosemite are covered in **deciduous** and **coniferous** forests. The highest **elevations** have alpine **ecosystems**. The Tuolumne River flows through high country in the northern part of the park. In the south, towering granite walls such as El Capitan and Half Dome rise above the Merced River in Yosemite Valley. This valley holds some of the tallest waterfalls in the world.

EL CAPITAN

3-IN-1

Yosemite Falls is made up of three separate waterfalls. It is the tallest waterfall in North America. It is 2,425 feet (739 meters) high!

AVERAGE TEMPERATURES

JANUARY
- ▲ HIGH: 48°F (9°C)
- ▼ LOW: 29°F (-2°C)

APRIL
- ▲ HIGH: 63°F (17°C)
- ▼ LOW: 38°F (3°C)

JULY
- ▲ HIGH: 89°F (32°C)
- ▼ LOW: 57°F (14°C)

OCTOBER
- ▲ HIGH: 71°F (22°C)
- ▼ LOW: 41°F (5°C)

°F = degrees Fahrenheit   °C = degrees Celsius

Yosemite has four seasons, with warm summers and cold winters. Snow often falls in the winter. Temperatures on the valley floor are usually warmer than higher elevations. In alpine regions, snow can last until late summer.

PLANTS AND WILDLIFE

Yosemite is filled with life! Black bears lumber through forests of ponderosa pines and white firs in the lower elevations. Lizards scamper over sun-soaked rocks in Yosemite Valley. Mule deer nibble grasses on the valley floor. They keep a lookout for predators such as coyotes and mountain lions.

Wildflowers such as harlequin lupine bring color to northern meadows at Hetch Hetchy. Trout swim in the area's **reservoir** and the park's rivers. In the southern part of the park, giant sequoias stretch to the sky. Tiny Douglas squirrels help these giants grow by spreading their seeds. Wood strawberries carpet the forest floor.

SIERRA FENCE LIZARD

MULE DEER

RAINBOW TROUT

COYOTE

DOUGLAS SQUIRREL

GROWING THROUGH FIRE

Wildfires help sequoias grow. The heat opens the sequoias' cones to release seeds. The fire also removes brush to give the seeds room to grow!

GIANT SEQUOIA

Life Span: more than 3,000 years
Status: endangered

giant sequoia range = ■

LEAST CONCERN	NEAR THREATENED	VULNERABLE	ENDANGERED	CRITICALLY ENDANGERED	EXTINCT IN THE WILD	EXTINCT

GREAT GRAY OWL

Life Span: up to 18 years
Status: least concern

great gray owl range = ■

LEAST CONCERN	NEAR THREATENED	VULNERABLE	ENDANGERED	CRITICALLY ENDANGERED	EXTINCT IN THE WILD	EXTINCT
▲						

Great gray owls swoop through red firs and lodgepole pines on Yosemite's higher slopes. Fishers also make homes in these forests. They hunt for porcupines hiding in the lodgepoles. Sapsuckers drill into the tall pines, searching for food.

Marmots chirp from rocks in Tuolumne Meadows. Alpine chipmunks scurry across the ground there. Wildflowers such as fireweed, gentians, and columbines add splashes of color between the grasses. Tree frogs call near lakes and streams. Sierra Nevada bighorn sheep skillfully climb Yosemite's tallest mountains, while peregrine falcons dive from the park's high cliffs.

NORTH AMERICAN FIREWEED

YELLOW-BELLIED MARMOT

HUMANS IN YOSEMITE NATIONAL PARK

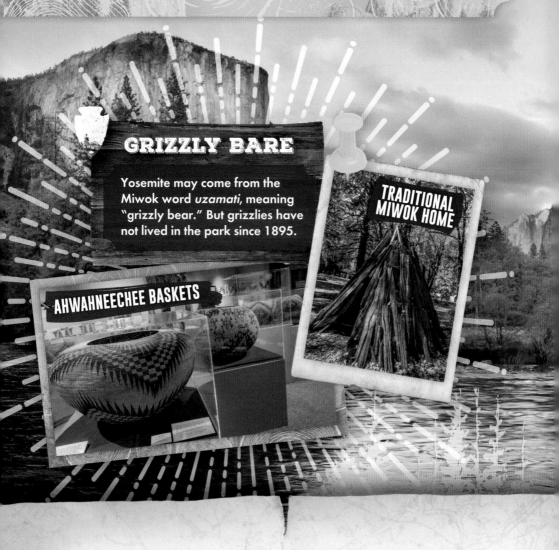

GRIZZLY BARE

Yosemite may come from the Miwok word *uzamati*, meaning "grizzly bear." But grizzlies have not lived in the park since 1895.

TRADITIONAL MIWOK HOME

AHWAHNEECHEE BASKETS

People have lived in Yosemite for thousands of years. For much of that time, groups moved in and out of Yosemite Valley with the seasons. Around 1400, a group of Southern Sierra Miwok Native Americans, the Ahwahneechee, permanently settled in the valley. They made baskets and gathered acorns and mushrooms. They also tended the land with fires to encourage growth.

The Ahwahneechee traded with other groups in the area.
The Paiutes lived nearby on the eastern side of the Sierras.
The Washoe lived to the north of Yosemite, the Yokuts lived to
the west, and the Western Mono lived to the southeast.

In 1851, the first group of white settlers, called the Mariposa Battalion, arrived in Yosemite Valley. They burned villages, and many Ahwahneechee were killed. Survivors of the attack were forced from the area.

Only a few years later, **tourists** came to view the beauty of the area. Soon, people wanted to protect the valley. In 1864, President Abraham Lincoln signed a law protecting Yosemite Valley and Mariposa Grove as a state park of California. In 1868, a **naturalist** named John Muir first visited Yosemite. Struck by its beauty, he felt it should be a national park. He wrote articles to convince others.

JOHN MUIR

PRESIDENT
BENJAMIN HARRISON

Muir's hard work paid off. In 1890, President Benjamin Harrison made Yosemite a national park. Then, in 1906, President Theodore Roosevelt expanded the park to include Yosemite Valley and Mariposa Grove.

During this time, Ahwahneechee, Paiute, and other Native Americans returned to the area. They lived and worked in the park for decades. But by 1970, they were forced out and their village was destroyed.

Today, Yosemite hosts more than 3 million visitors each year. No Native Americans live in the park. Some hold ceremonies or gatherings at the park's reconstructed Indian Village. Visitors can tour the village and learn about Native American **cultures**.

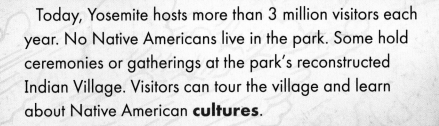

CABIN IN INDIAN VILLAGE

A HIDDEN VALLEY

In 1906, a dam was planned at Hetch Hetchy Valley. It would flood the valley and form a reservoir. John Muir thought the valley was too beautiful to flood and fought against the dam. He was unsuccessful.

VISITING YOSEMITE NATIONAL PARK

Yosemite offers many fun activities! Rock climbers flock to the park to tackle its granite cliffs. Hikers take to the many trails including the steep yet popular Half Dome. Families swim or raft in the Merced River. Visitors to the Yosemite Museum can learn about basket weaving and other Native American arts, and may even see a **demonstration**.

ROCK CLIMBING

FIREFALL AT HORSETAIL FALLS

FIREFALL

People who visit the park in February might catch a glimpse of Yosemite's famous Firefall. At sunset, the light hits Horsetail Falls just right to make it glow red and orange!

HALF DOME

MAJESTIC YOSEMITE HOTEL

MARIPOSA GROVE

YOSEMITE FALLS

In winter, people can ice skate at a rink in Yosemite Valley. Snowshoers and cross-country skiers take advantage of many trails throughout the park. Downhill skiers, snowboarders, and snow tubers can enjoy the slopes at Badger Pass ski area.

PROTECTING THE PARK

Human use has threatened Yosemite for decades. Air pollution is one of the biggest threats to the park today. It comes from cars, factories, and the nearby Central Valley. It can make the air hazy and harm people and wildlife. Wildfires also affect the air quality in the park.

Climate change worsens many of the threats to the park. Warming temperatures make **droughts** more common. Without snow and rainfall, many of Yosemite's most spectacular features, like its waterfalls and the Merced River, will dry up. Climate change also affects homes for wildlife, pushing animals to higher elevations.

DROUGHT

WILDFIRE SMOKE

People are working to protect Yosemite. The park has made many changes to reduce climate change and air pollution within the park. Shuttles take visitors around the valley to limit car use. **Solar panels** provide clean energy for some of the park.

SOLAR PANEL

Scientists are studying the changes happening within the park. They learn how to better combat threats. Rangers are already using what they have learned to help the park. Teams manage wildfires to maintain healthy ecosystems. Others work on removing harmful **invasive species**. Their work can protect the park for many years to come!

YOSEMITE NATIONAL PARK FACTS

Area: **1,190** square miles
(3,082 square kilometers)

Annual Visitors:
3,343,998 visitors in 2021

Area Rank: **16**TH
largest park

Population Rank: **8**TH
most visited park in 2021

Date Established:
October 1, 1890

Highest point: Mount Lyell;
13,114 feet (3,997 meters)

TIMELINE

AROUND 1400

Ahwahneechee people settle in Yosemite Valley

1851

Ahwahneechee people are forcibly removed from the valley in an attack by the Mariposa Battalion

FOOD WEB

FISHER

COYOTE

PORCUPINE

DOUGLAS SQUIRREL

ALPINE CHIPMUNK

SEQUOIA SEEDS

LODGEPOLE PINES

WOOD STRAWBERRIES

1864

President Lincoln makes Yosemite Valley and Mariposa Grove the first state park in the world

YOSEMITE NATIONAL PARK

1906

President Theodore Roosevelt adds Yosemite Valley and Mariposa Grove to the national park

1890

President Harrison signs Yosemite National Park into law

GLOSSARY

alpine—related to high areas of mountains

climate change—a human-caused change in Earth's weather due to warming temperatures

coniferous—related to trees and bushes that are evergreen, have needle-like leaves, and bear cones instead of seeds

cultures—beliefs, arts, and ways of life in places or societies

deciduous—related to trees that lose their leaves each year

demonstration—an act of showing how something is done

droughts—long periods of dry weather

ecosystems—communities of living things that include plants, animals, and the environments around them

elevations—heights above sea level

erosion—the process through which rocks are worn away by wind, water, or ice

glaciers—massive sheets of ice that cover large areas of land

intrusions—events in which melted rock pushes up through other rock layers or formations

invasive species—plants or animals that are not originally from the area; invasive species often cause harm to their new environments.

metamorphic—related to a type of rock that forms from heat and pressure

naturalist—a person who studies nature

reservoir—a human-made body of water

sedimentary—related to a type of rock that forms from layers of sediment that are pressed together; sediments are tiny pieces of rocks, minerals, and other natural materials.

solar panels—devices that turn sunlight into energy

tourists—people who travel to visit another place

TO LEARN MORE

AT THE LIBRARY

Oachs, Emily Rose. *California*. Minneapolis, Minn.: Bellwether Media, 2022.

Payne, Stefanie. *The National Parks: Discover All 62 Parks of the United States*. New York, N.Y.: DK Publishing, 2020.

Perritano, John. *Yosemite*. New York, N.Y.: AV2 by Weigl, 2019.

ON THE WEB

FACTSURFER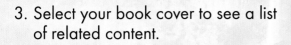

Factsurfer.com gives you a safe, fun way to find more information.

1. Go to www.factsurfer.com.

2. Enter "Yosemite National Park" into the search box and click 🔍.

3. Select your book cover to see a list of related content.

INDEX